T0353193

KELLIE SMITH

Kellie Smith was shortlisted for the Bruntwood Prize for Playwriting and awarded a residency at the Royal Exchange Theatre, Manchester, and Liverpool Everyman, where she wrote her plays *Black Gold* and *The Sum of Parts*. She has written many plays for young people, most recently *The Monstrum* for NT Connections. Her short film *The Big Day* won BIFA's Best Short Film Award, whilst her half-hour drama, *To Know Him* earned her a RTS nomination for Best Screenwriter. Kellie's Radio 4 afternoon plays include *Can't Live Without You*, *Homeowners* and *The Archivist*.

Kellie Smith

WILDERNESS

NICK HERN BOOKS

London

www.nickhernbooks.co.uk

A Nick Hern Book

Wilderness first published in Great Britain as a paperback original in 2019 by Nick Hern Books Limited, The Glasshouse, 49a Goldhawk Road, London W12 8QP

Wilderness copyright © 2019 Kellie Smith

Kellie Smith has asserted her right to be identified as the author of this work

Cover image © istockphoto.com/wildpixel

Designed and typeset by Nick Hern Books, London
Printed in Great Britain by Mimeo Ltd, Huntingdon, Cambridgeshire PE29 6XX

A CIP catalogue record for this book is available from the British Library

ISBN 978 1 84842 833 1

Wilderness was first performed at Hampstead Theatre
Downstairs, London, on 21 March 2019. The cast was as follows:

ALAN/PETER/POLICEMAN   Richard Frame
ANNE   Natalie Klamar
STEPHANIE/NEIGHBOUR/   Allison McKenzie
  CAFCASS OFFICER
JOE   Finlay Robertson

Director   Anna Ledwich
Designer   Lucy Sierra
Lighting Designer   Matt Haskins
Sound Designer   Dan Balfour

'No one ever died from a snake bite'

Wayne Dyer

Characters

ANNE
JOE
STEPH / NEIGHBOUR / CAFCASS OFFICER
POLICEMAN / PETER / ALAN

Note on Play

The opening and end speeches are completely open to interpretation. They may be said by any number of characters or someone else entirely. In the original production the prologue was spoken by Anne and Joe and the epilogue was cut. The epilogue is included here as an optional addition to the play.

/ indicates an overlap.

– indicates either an unfinished thought or a 'take-up' from another character's unfinished thought.

This is intended purely as a guide and also because I like to write as I hear it. Please don't feel wedded to the syntax.

This text went to press before the end of rehearsals and so may differ slightly from the play as performed.

Sometimes –

Sometimes –

People just fall out of love.

There might not be any big reason why.

It just happens.

They still like each other but they don't love each other any more.

Love is like a plant, you see. It needs watering. And if you don't water it –

You have to look after your love, and we didn't.

We did other things –

And then one day we realised our love was gone –

It had disappeared –

And that made us feel angry, and sad –

Because we couldn't get it back, no matter how hard we tried.

We weren't 'in love' with each other any more.

But that doesn't mean we love you any less.

Because our love for you could never ever go away.

It's a different sort of love.

It's not a love that needs watering –

It's more like a tree. A very strong tree.

A tree that can withstand any storm.

This isn't your fault. You mustn't think that you've done anything wrong.

We've both decided this is for the best.

We won't argue now.

We'll be happier now.

Things are going to be better.

Daddy won't be living here any more, but will be here as much as possible still.

In time, this will just be normal.

Lots of children have two homes.

Lots of children have mummies and daddies that don't live in the same place.

Daddy's going to get you a spaceman bed at his place.

Paint planets on your wall.

You'll have two bedrooms. That's exciting isn't it?

Your room's going to be really special.

You'll get to spend time with us both, one on one.

Everything is going to be okay.

We promise.

We love you.

We love you more than anything in the world, and that's bigger than anything else.

That's bigger than this.

New Year's Eve. Town on a Saturday night. JOE *is running up a road, dragging* STEPH *behind him. She's amused but slightly bewildered.*

STEPH. What's going on? Joe? *Joe* –

JOE. Think we can get a taxi up here.

STEPH. We didn't even say goodbye?

JOE. You know what's it like – they'll be all – 'No, no, no – '

STEPH. We're going to miss the countdown –

JOE. We'll do our own countdown –

STEPH. What's his name? He was getting us a drink –

JOE. It doesn't matter –

STEPH. This just feels a bit –

JOE. I'll message them now – I'll say we had a bloody great time – but you're driving to your mum's tomorrow –

STEPH. You're not blaming me.

JOE. I'll say you've got the shits.

STEPH. I thought we were going to dance. Joe?

We hear music from a bar – 'I would walk five hundred miles' –

Ohhhhh. Love this. Love this song.

She's trying to get him to dance to it.

Come.

JOE. No –

STEPH. Come on –

She's dancing, for a moment JOE *seems distracted by the song.*

JOE. I hate town.

STEPH. It's New Year's Eve –

JOE. Exactly

STEPH. I finally get to meet your friends –

JOE. They're just people that I met in school, that I'm still friends with out of pure laziness –

STEPH. I liked them –

JOE. They'll be dragging us to Reflex or some shite next –

STEPH. You said you'd lost touch – you wanted to make an effort –

JOE. I enjoyed the meal. That was enough.

STEPH. Really?

JOE. And you.

He pulls her in.

I'm so bloody proud of you. I am. Everyone proper loved you. You're just so easy – you get on with everyone. I'd just rather be with you, Steph – than sat in some sweaty bar listening to Pritchard walk me through his garage conversion – his favorite fucking podcasts.

She's disappointed.

I'm sorry. I just find them all a bit –

STEPH. I didn't know you were having that bad a time.

JOE. Cheese chips, gravy – Jools Holland?

Beat.

I'll even wear my Christmas pyjamas.

STEPH. Fine.

JOE. Thank you.

STEPH. You weirdo.

JOE. I've got a bag of Chilli Doritos with your name on it.

STEPH. Sounds amazing.

JOE. Do you mind?

STEPH. No.

JOE. Let's just walk to the cobbles – Way too busy here.

They start walking –

STEPH. Oh shit.

JOE. What?

STEPH. I've left my cardigan.

JOE. Cardigan?

STEPH. My grey one – the pearls – I'll just run back –

JOE. Just leave it –

STEPH. I'll just nip in –

JOE. It's just a cardigan, it doesn't matter –

STEPH. It's under the table, I can just grab it –

JOE. No –

STEPH. It won't take me five minutes –

JOE. I'll buy you a new one.

STEPH. Why?

JOE. Because I just want to go.

STEPH. You're being really –

JOE. I don't want to see them again.

STEPH. I'll go –

JOE. *No, Steph –*

STEPH. Why not?

>*Beat.*

>What is it?

>*She eyes him.*

>Has something happened? What?

>*Beat.*

JOE. Look. Just – hear me out. Fuck's sake.

>*Beat.*

>My ex is in there.

STEPH. – Your ex?

JOE. She just walked in. I didn't know she was out – she must have got a sitter –

STEPH. – Anne?

JOE. Yes.

STEPH. Anne is in there?

JOE. Yes.

STEPH. That's what all this – ?

Beat.

– Did she see us?

JOE. I don't – maybe –

STEPH. Joe?

JOE. I just didn't want –

STEPH. Fucking hell?

JOE. A – thing –

STEPH. You just dragged me out?

JOE. She'd be straight over to us –

STEPH. Well, yeah –

JOE. You don't know –

STEPH. It's going to look really fucking odd.

JOE. I panicked.

STEPH. We have to go back.

JOE. No, no, no –

STEPH. We have to.

JOE. No –

STEPH. I know we've been avoiding this –

JOE. She probably didn't see –

STEPH. But it's another thing blanking her – doing a runner? You said – she's been asking to meet me?

JOE. You're not meeting her.

STEPH. Joe –

JOE. You want to be stood there on the countdown – *with Anne*?

STEPH. She isn't going to let me meet Ally.

Beat.

Isn't that what you said? She wants you to introduce me first – ?

JOE. Look. Look here's the thing – I have said – I have made it clear – it's up to me – I didn't vet any of her boyfriends.

STEPH. Have any of them met him yet?

Beat.

I know – I know it's utter bullshit –

JOE. No – God –

STEPH. It's going to be weird and awkward –

JOE. I can't –

STEPH. But you want me to meet your son don't you?

JOE. Course. I'm desperate for you –

STEPH. Then I say we just get this shit over with.

JOE. You're being really fucking cool about this – and that's great. In fact, it just makes me love you even more but –

STEPH *looks at him*.

What?

She is trying not to smile.

What?

STEPH. – You haven't actually said –

JOE. You know I do –

STEPH. *That* –

JOE. Is that okay? Is that okay if I say that?

STEPH. Yeah.

JOE. I love you.

STEPH. Love you too.

A moment.

They kiss.

JOE. See? This is us – this is – These past few months – perfect. You're perfect. And I just don't want her – this isn't to do with her.

STEPH. I just don't want to cause any problems –

JOE. There's no problem –

STEPH. But if this is something –

JOE. It's not happening, all right?

Beat.

I'm sorry – I just – Every little thing with Anne. My every move – ever since he was a baby. Don't let go of his hand – don't feed him that. Where are you taking him? Have I ever hurt him? Have I ever done anything – ? I'm not with her any more. Okay? I'm out of that shit. And this – it's just about respect – her respecting my choices. I don't like being – This isn't up to her. It's really – it's not.

Beat.

STEPH. I thought you said things were okay between you now?

JOE. They are – it's fine. It's as good as it's ever going to be.

He takes a breath.

You have to trust me on this. If I give in to her on this – then that'll be it. Pandora's box. We'll never be rid of her.

STEPH. – Okay.

JOE. I'm sorry.

STEPH. No – I understand –

JOE. I already feel like this has tainted –

STEPH. Joe.

JOE. I don't want you to think –

STEPH. It's okay. It's not like I *want* to meet her –

JOE. God, no.

STEPH. I just –

Beat.

Do you think she saw me?

JOE. I don't know.

STEPH. I'm all – my hair –

JOE. You look beautiful.

STEPH. I don't care.

Beat.

Just – don't do that again.

JOE. What?

STEPH. We decide things together – okay?

JOE. Okay.

He holds her.

I just want things – want this – always like this.

They kiss.

Fireworks go off in the distance.

The bar music swells.

STEPH. Let's go.

JOE. Let's run.

He's jokingly pulling her along. She laughs.

STEPH. Joe

JOE. I'm getting out of here – before you change your mind –

STEPH. *Joe –*

Only laughter disappearing up the street.

We see only ANNE. *She has two coffees in her hand. She's looking at something on a nearby wall.*

ANNE. So – there we are. Hurtling down the dock road. And it's happened so fast. I mean, I woke up with what I thought was Braxton Hicks at about 2 a.m. and by 3 a.m., I've got contractions which are three minutes apart. I couldn't even walk across the car park. Thought I'm going to give birth on the reception floor. And Joe's forgotten the medical book – the maternity-record thingy and he's arguing with the girl behind reception because she won't book me in without it and he's like 'Do you want her to have this baby now? Right now – on your desk?' I'm whipped through – eight centimetres and the baby is coming. He's coming all right. No time for drugs. No time for the inflatable ball. No time for anything. 'Push, push, push, push.' His head is stuck. Couldn't get his head past my bloody pelvis. I'm in all sort of positions. Rocking back and forth. They're trying to manoeuver his head. Ugh. Excruciating. Cut me twice. Finally forceps – And I'm in too much pain to care. 'Just get him out. Get him out.' And suddenly he is – he's out – But – nothing – couldn't hear anything. The whole room – sort of shifts. Suddenly there are doctors and oxygen and I couldn't see – 'What's happening? Where's my baby? What's going on?' A doctor. This woman – grey streak – never forget her – she's trying to calm me down – and finally she says 'What did you call him?'

Beat.

I say 'Alistair'. She says 'I'm so sorry, Alistair is gone.'

Beat.

I – I wanted to hold him. I knew that straight away. I just – knew. 'Give me my baby.' Made them. Opened my top, and I lay Alistair on me. His tiny – tiny body. Our hot tears. I hold him and I say –

Alistair, your bedroom is blue and yellow.

Alistair, you live on Langley Road.

Alistair, it's nearly Easter.

Alistair, I call you peanut.

You like UB40.

You have your daddy's chin.

Alistair –

Alistair –

Alistair –

Something flickers in the room.

Joe saw it first. His little body, lifting and falling – just slightly –

This opens out.

We're in a treatment room of a Wellbeing Centre.

STEPH *is still at her desk listening. The door is slightly open.*

STEPH. – That's incredible.

ANNE. They've done lots of research into it – They've done studies – the way that the mother's brain lights up when the child's in distress. I read this one thing about how your kids, all the kids that you'll ever have, leave, literally leave traces of themselves – like their DNA – in your brain. So all that instinct, all that intuition –

STEPH. Wow.

ANNE. It's all proven. It's all in there.

STEPH. That's – wow.

ANNE. They got some air into his lungs and two weeks later we carried our perfect baby out the hospital doors, feeling like we'd just cheated death.

Beat.

Hard to believe – eight years ago.

ANNE *drinks her coffee.*

STEPH *watches her.*

STEPH. Anne – So sorry. It's just I've got a full diary –

ANNE. Receptionist said you're on lunch now?

STEPH. They just let you through?

ANNE. Just chanced it. Thought 'I bet that's the place.' Looks like a travel agents' from outside –

STEPH. It's a Wellbeing Centre.

ANNE. Right, right.

STEPH. Holistic therapy.

ANNE. Alternative medicine.

STEPH. Reflexology, Reiki –

ANNE. Yes – that's it – the Reiki.

STEPH. – Yes.

ANNE. What is – that?

STEPH. It's Japanese – stress-reduction –

ANNE. Mm.

STEPH. It promotes healing –

ANNE. I see.

STEPH. Through the hands –

ANNE. Like a massage?

STEPH. Actually clients keep their clothes on.

Beat.

It's based on the idea that we all have an unseen life-force energy – that flows around the body – And sometimes – sometimes – that energy can be low – or it can be disrupted –

ANNE. Disrupted?

STEPH. Sometimes it needs to be cleared or healed to flow in a healthy, natural way again.

ANNE. And you can do that?

STEPH. Yes.

ANNE. With your hands?

STEPH. We all can. We all do. Every time you put your hands where someone hurts – Like you. Like your – your birth story.

Beat.

I actually don't really take a lunch –

ANNE. Oh, look at me. I bought you a coffee too.

ANNE *gives it to* STEPH.

Don't worry about it. Just popped next door.

STEPH. – Thanks.

ANNE. / Didn't know if you'd just be into all the herbal stuff. I'm trying to cut down. Four flat whites a day. That's too much isn't it?

STEPH. The thing is, Anne. I am – I'm kind of in work right now.

Beat.

ANNE. Oh.

STEPH. Yeah.

ANNE. Is this not okay?

STEPH. Well –

ANNE. Gosh. I am so sorry.

STEPH. No – It's all right.

ANNE. I just thought, I'll just say a quick 'hello'.

STEPH. And it's so nice to meet you, finally –

ANNE. Well, that's it. I thought we're never going to meet if one of us doesn't make the first move.

STEPH. It's just I don't really have visitors –

ANNE. I was just passing. Thought 'I'll poke my head in'.

STEPH. And that's lovely, and the coffee too –

ANNE. Because it feels like it's gone on for a bit, us not meeting.

STEPH. Yes –

ANNE. And I know last weekend you met Alistair.

STEPH. – I did – And he's lovely. He really is.

ANNE. So I just thought, we need to meet now really. Don't we?

Beat.

Important. When you think about it.

Beat.

STEPH. I've got ten minutes.

ANNE. If we wait for Joe to introduce us, hell will freeze.

STEPH *is shutting the door.*

Fingers in ears. 'La la la.' That's the Joe method. And you know what? I thought, what's the problem here? We're all adults.

STEPH. Of course.

ANNE. Why can't we just sit down?

STEPH. Sit down?

ANNE. Talk about what's best for Alistair.

STEPH. What do you mean?

ANNE. Sometimes it's best if the women do it. That's what it takes.

STEPH. I'm not sure – ?

ANNE. Okay. Okay. Here's the thing.

Beat.

Joe didn't say he was planning on introducing you – just yet.

STEPH. Okay – ?

ANNE. You see?

STEPH. Well – It wasn't planned.

ANNE. I mean those sorts of things – we need to decide together –

STEPH. I was just popping in because I'd left my gym shorts at Joe's –

ANNE. Right.

STEPH. And Alistair was there. Joe just said I was 'Daddy's friend', and that was fine. He was totally fine.

ANNE. Do you stay over at Joe's?

STEPH. – Well – yes –

ANNE. So your things are there? I just mean – Alistair isn't stupid.

STEPH. Of course not. I think we just felt if we don't make a big thing of it, then it won't be a big thing.

ANNE. Can I talk honestly to you?

STEPH. – Okay?

ANNE. Because I think it is best, if we are honest, from the beginning. So important in these situations. Don't you think?

STEPH. – Yes –

ANNE. I'm happy for Joe. Really I am. And you seem lovely – I'm sure you're good for him. I'm sure you're just what he needs. Are your parents still together?

STEPH. Sorry?

ANNE. Do you mind me asking?

STEPH. – Yes. They are.

ANNE. My parents split up. I wasn't much younger than Alistair is now. It was a very – a very volatile situation. I suppose that what's made me determined, absolutely determined to keep a really positive relationship with Joe – For Alistair – Our priority has to be him. Do you know what I mean?

STEPH. Of course.

ANNE. It's all about mutual respect – communication. Communication is key. There's no reason why Joe and I can't get along – if we listen to each other. If we respect each other's wishes. No reason at all. Because – the thing is – And I'm not sure if you're aware of this – but I did make my feelings clear on this one – I said – I explained – I didn't want him to introduce Alistair to you yet.

Beat.

STEPH. Oh.

ANNE. I said I just felt it was too soon. Far too soon actually. I asked him to wait. And yet – he's gone ahead. And I know – you say it 'wasn't planned' and you were just 'popping in' but – you must have known that Alistair was there –

STEPH. Well –

ANNE. What I'm saying is it could have been avoided, and what I feel – what I feel is – it's opened a door. The door is open now. And it's going to happen again and again and 'Daddy's friend' becomes 'Daddy's girlfriend' and I'm afraid Alistair is just not ready for that. He's just not.

Beat.

STEPH. Look. If it helps – Ally – He was –

ANNE. Alistair.

STEPH. Sorry –?

ANNE. It's Alistair.

STEPH. He – was really bubbly. Chatty. We even ended up on the trampoline. He was showing me how to do front-flips.

ANNE. – Front-flips?

STEPH. And I was a bit nervous about meeting him but it went well. It went really well.

ANNE. – I thought you said you'd just 'popped in'?

STEPH. – Yes –

ANNE. But you were nervous about 'meeting him'?

STEPH. I just mean – when it happened –

ANNE. Right.

STEPH. Anne. I can assure you. He was totally – *totally* fine.

ANNE. Was he?

STEPH. Yes.

Beat.

ANNE. I don't know how to put this. I'm not saying that Joe doesn't – it's something about boys and their fathers. Alistair's always trying to seem tough in front of his dad. When he came home last weekend – he was very quiet. Not himself at all and it wasn't until bedtime that he told me what happened. There was this woman at his dad's house. He was confused. You know the thing he was most worried about?

STEPH. Worried?

ANNE. Is she going to be there every weekend now? Will I still see my dad? I've tried to reassure him. I've done my best. I've called Joe – it's like talking to the wall. That's why I'm here. I'm hoping that you will see –

Beat.

All kids like this, they dream about their parents getting back together. Meeting you – that was the end of that dream for Alistair.

Beat.

STEPH. You've been split up for over a year –

ANNE. It doesn't matter.

Beat.

STEPH. Look. Anne. If this is about what happened – New Year's Eve?

ANNE. I don't care about that –

STEPH. Because it did seem like you were pissed off at the time?

ANNE. I wasn't 'pissed off' –

STEPH. Well maybe a bit annoyed? The text messages you sent –

ANNE. Of course it felt odd –

STEPH. Of course –

ANNE. Immature –

STEPH. You're right. You are. But it's good that we're meeting now. Because if I'm going to be a part of Joe's life, then it makes sense going forwards that we do know who each other are.

Pause.

ANNE. You know, it's funny. Here. This room.

Beat.

Can't quite picture it. Can't picture – Joe – coming here.

Beat.

Couldn't even bear his feet being touched. I started doing morning yoga once. You'd think I'd joined a cult.

She laughs.

He was never into – all this.

STEPH. I wouldn't say –

ANNE. But he came here? This is where you met?

STEPH. – Well no – yes – professionally – I was working –

ANNE. I know.

STEPH. I didn't bump into him again – till weeks later –

ANNE. He told me.

Pause.

I want to say something to you, Steph.

She hesitates.

Nobody expects a relationship to fail. Do you know what I mean? It's just sometimes. Sometimes –

Beat.

He told me that he went to his GP at the time – he said – he needed to speak to someone. I mean men his age – they don't go to the doctor – They don't ask for help. You'd think they'd take him seriously. Six-month waiting list to see a counsellor. He must have been so desperate to come here – *this* –

Beat.

I'm sorry – I didn't mean it like that.

Beat.

I just mean – just because I was the one that ended things –
that doesn't mean I didn't feel it too. But – Now? Nothing
but happiness to see Joe – to see him – better. We have this
beautiful, beautiful little boy and that's all that matters.
That's all that counts – Whatever else.

Beat.

When you're a mum – You'll get it.

ANNE *gets her things together.*

Lovely to meet you at last.

STEPH. You too.

They smile.

ANNE. Enjoy your coffee.

ANNE *leaves.*

After a moment, STEPH *puts her coffee in the bin.*

ANNE *has a suitcase.*

She opens it, and begins putting things in it.

ANNE. Socks
    Underpants
    Vests
    T-shirts
    Hoodie
    Jeans
    Shorts – just in case. I don't know if football was mentioned.
    Pyjamas. I got you some new pyjamas. I'll pull the tags out.
    This is your soap bag. There's toothbrush. Flannel. Eczema
    cream – You have to remember this – twice a day.
    And that's everything. That's it.

So – exciting.

Are you excited?

You look excited. You should be. I bet this Saturday is going to be jam-packed. I bet Daddy has so much planned. Going to be brilliant isn't it? He's bought in all your favorite things. Coco Pops, Pop Tarts. Lucky boy. Boys only. Boys' rules, this weekend.

She shuts the case.

She opens the case.

She unpacks.

Look at this stuff, all neatly folded. Wow-wee. Did you pack this or did Daddy? All freshly washed. Well done Daddy. Is that chewing gum? Did you have chewing gum? I'll have to soak that. Have you noticed how clean the house is? Mummy spent all evening cleaning. I even scrubbed the patio. You'll never guess what I found? I found a little black frog hiding underneath the bin. And you wouldn't believe it – I managed to capture him and put him in a jar with some water, and twigs. I was so impressed with myself. Then when I was bringing him inside, I tripped on the step. Smashed the jar – everywhere. The bloody thing escaped. Hopping all over the kitchen. Should have heard me, Alistair, screaming the place down I was. I was thinking, where's my brave boy when I need him?

She shuts the case.

ANNE *opens the case.*

She packs.

I'm going to let you take Pinky, Alistair, but you have to look after him, keep him safe okay? He smells of Mummy's fabric softener. Pinky's a little bit nervous about spending a whole weekend away from home but I've told him that you're going to look after him. You're going to be brave. And if he wants to call home, you're going to call home for him. And if Pinky misses Mummy, I've told him that all he needs to do is hold on to you. Hold on to you tight.

She shuts the case.

She opens the case, unpacks.

Who packed this bag?

Did Daddy make you pack it?

Look at this.

She smells the clothes.

Everything needs washing.

Where are your shoes?

Did Daddy pack your school shoes?

She looks. They're not there.

What are you going to wear on your feet tomorrow?

And look at your arms. Alistair? Your arms – They're red raw. They'll be itching you tonight. We'll have to put twice as much on. It's going to sting.

What's this?

She takes out a piece of scrunched-up paper and reads it.

Homework.

It's seven o' clock on a Sunday evening.

It's –

She counts to ten.

Do you know what I have been doing this weekend? I have been working. I have gone back to doing nights. There are blisters all over my feet, I have someone's sick on my shoulder, and I haven't had that since you were a baby.

She breathes.

It's fine. It's fine.

There are things going on right now. Things I can't tell you. So sometimes, I need you. I need you on my side. Do you understand?

Pause.

She looks in the bag.

Where's Pinky? Alistair?

Alistair.

Pinky lives here.

She shuts the case.

The woods.

JOE *and* STEPH *are trekking, backpacks on.*

STEPH. It's like overnight they're somehow transformed –
that's the word – to some higher state – do you know what
I mean? Like suddenly they're this celestial being. All these
quotes about this sacred bond – about how they're now the
most important – special – amazing life form to grace this
earth. How much they love, love, love their children. Yes –
you're supposed to love your kid. It would be really weird if
you didn't love your kid. Congratulations you've spawned
and you don't want to commit filicide. You still pissed in a
bedroom drawer once. You know? It's like a club.
Sometimes I think it's some elitist club. Because isn't it *so*
hard? Don't we work *so* hard? So much harder than anyone
without kids could possibly – *possibly* understand. Us mere
mortals cannot possibly fathom the life-changing experience
of shitty bums. Screaming at their kids in Primark then
posting pictures about how motherhood is the 'greatest gift'.
You know? Do you know?

JOE. Yeah.

STEPH. Some of us don't actually want kids. Some people have
fucked-up wombs –

JOE. Fucked-up wombs –

STEPH. What's wrong with saying that?

JOE. No, no it's just not something I thought I'd hear –

STEPH. / It needs to be said –

JOE. On this trip –

STEPH. A little perspective that's all. Not being a mother doesn't make me subhuman and becoming a mother doesn't mean you belong to some divine species. I parked in a parent-and-child spot once. I didn't realise – and this woman, this woman she looked at me – pure hatred. I'm just so glad that we don't feel the pressure.

JOE. Me too.

STEPH. That means a lot to me actually. I don't think that being a woman in my thirties means that my every relationship –

JOE. Your 'every' relationship?

STEPH. *This* relationship. It has to be based in – in – in truth. On the fact that we love each other and we want to be together –

JOE. Of course –

STEPH. I'm not in love with your sperm.

JOE. Okay.

STEPH. I'm not weighing up your sperm count –

JOE. Good to know.

STEPH. Even if you had no balls, I would still love you.

JOE. That's – great.

JOE has stopped.

STEPH. What?

JOE. I love you too.

He kisses her.

He begins clearing away bits of tree branches in the clearing they have arrived at.

STEPH. What are you doing?

JOE. We're here.

She looks around. Eventually JOE *clears away the debris to reveal a small man-made shelter. He looks at* STEPH *for a reaction.*

STEPH. – So?

JOE. Yeah, so yeah.

They look.

Huge isn't it?

STEPH. – This is – it?

JOE. This is it.

Beat.

STEPH. Is it – It's like a den?

JOE *takes away some more camouflage.*

JOE. No, it's not a den. It's not a den, Steph. It's a shelter. It's a whole wooden structure. These are all twelve-feet poles, cut from trees around here. All the sides are covered with tree branches – they sort of act like the ribs. Tons of debris on the sides so it's camouflaged. That's all heavy-duty rope. Heavy-duty tarp covering. The lean-to – that's where the beds are. Made a bough bed.

STEPH. A bough bed?

JOE. It's actually incredibly comfy. I've used very thick poles there. There's a smoke hole. First-aid kit. There's even a little underground hatch.

STEPH *stares at it.*

You could say something.

STEPH. I think – I thought – I pictured – a cabin?

JOE. A cabin?

STEPH. Or bunkhouse – sort of thing?

JOE. I made this Steph.

STEPH. And – It's –

JOE. I made it all on my own.

STEPH. Wow. Incredible.

JOE. You need to see inside – come have a look.

She pokes her head in. Spits out a cobweb.

Pretty amazing – ?

STEPH. Small but –

JOE. Functional.

STEPH. We're quite exposed – ?

JOE. Oh no – this is the best bit.

He brings down a tarpaulin covering.

Snug as a bug.

STEPH. What about animals – ?

JOE. That's why I have the hatch. I put all our food down there.

STEPH. You've slept here before?

JOE. Loads –

STEPH. We're protected aren't we? From the animals –

JOE. Steph –

STEPH. And you know – people?

JOE. There are no people.

STEPH. No.

JOE. We are completely 'off-grid'. You didn't even know it was here.

STEPH. No –

JOE. Did you? We were right on it and you didn't know –

STEPH. / This was it.

JOE. It was here.

Pause.

You do like it?

STEPH. Oh – yeah.

He starts unpacking.

JOE. I've wanted to bring you here for so long. Just wanted to get straight. Fix it up a bit first.

STEPH. You fixed it up?

JOE. Replaced some of the rope – reframed some of the inside – just clearing all the debris. We've had a pretty rough winter, you know?

STEPH. Yeah it's been – rough.

She notices him watching her.

Excited.

JOE. You could start collecting some wood – or something?

STEPH. Right, yeah.

JOE. I'll just do a little recce of the place.

She begins picking up pieces.

Dry pieces. Ash wood works best. First rule of making a fire. Contrary to popular belief fuel wood doesn't need to look like those huge logs you put on your fireplace. Branches as wide as your wrist or your forearm are fine.

STEPH. Got it.

JOE. Oh – almost forgot.

He rummages inside his bag. Throws her a walkie-talkie.

STEPH. What's this?

JOE (*speaking into his*). Do you copy?

He indicates for her to switch hers on, which she does.

STEPH. – Hello?

JOE. What's your ten-twenty?

STEPH. – What's my?

JOE. Location.

STEPH. Here?

JOE. That's a negative –

STEPH. – Base camp?

JOE. Roger. Over and out.

She's staring at him.

Case we're separated.

STEPH. Can't I just shout – ?

JOE. Shout?

STEPH. Or phone – ?

JOE. Steph?

STEPH. I can still get a signal –

JOE. Steph.

STEPH. What?

JOE. If this was a SHTF situation –

STEPH. A what?

JOE. 'Shit Hits The Fan?'

She stares at him.

Natural disaster – Outbreak – A solar flare –

STEPH. Solar flare – ?

JOE. If a solar storm hit us – all our technology would be wiped out. The entire planet would go dark.

STEPH. This isn't some post-apocalyptic wet dream is it?

JOE. This is survival skills, Steph. This is what they should be teaching kids. Everyone.

STEPH. That's why you made this?

JOE. / Everyone should have at least a basic understanding of bushcraft.

STEPH. In case the world ends?

JOE. What? No –

STEPH. Is that what this is for?

JOE. I made it for Ally.

Beat.

STEPH. Right.

JOE. Even though he hasn't been yet. God knows why I don't just bring him. Just wanted to get it right. Don't want to put him off it. Started with some of the easy stuff. He's got into that. Showed him how to cook an egg on a fire using just a stick the other week – he was brilliant. Something we can share, you know? Coming here. Proper father–son. When I was a kid, spend all day out building dens, jumping in rivers, climbing trees. Come home with scraped knees – ripped jeans. I could name every plant, every tree, every bird. I don't know. You lose touch with these things.

STEPH. – Anne wasn't in to – all this?

JOE. God no.

He's laughing to himself.

No.

JOE carries on sorting things out.

STEPH *is watching him.*

STEPH. You know – so funny. Did I tell you this? When she came to see me. It was almost like she was trying to imply – well no – she was sort of directly saying – Telling me how devastated you were – over her.

She laughs.

JOE. – God.

STEPH. *I know.* Telling me? All I wanted to say – fuck. Woman. He hates your guts. Can you not see that?

JOE. Madness.

STEPH. She has this completely deluded picture in her head. Well yeah. You told me she was mad as a box of frogs but it's only seeing it.

JOE. Well it's not going to happen again, so –

STEPH. I feel sorry for her. In truth I do. Because some people – some people just have a lot going on inside of them – and they have zero awareness about it and it's sad – it's actually sad to watch. You're going to have to be careful. So careful with how you handle her.

JOE. I've said – I'll have words.

STEPH. No, no – I don't want you to. I really don't. It's done now. And I think I handled it really well. We've just got to keep her at arm's length –

JOE. Yeah.

STEPH. It's just about boundaries –

JOE. Well let's just leave talking about her.

STEPH. I'm not talking about her.

JOE. This is our weekend – right?

STEPH. I just want to say – people like her. You just can't let them in. You just have to be strict with yourself, Joe.

JOE. I do. I am.

STEPH. Don't let her call all the time. She calls all the time.

JOE. I've told her to just text –

STEPH. It's like we'll be sitting down to watch a film – even going to bed. Having sex. (*Makes the sound of his ringtone.*)

JOE. I try to remember – put your phone on silent –

STEPH. And it's like she has to knock at the door every time she picks Ally up and spend ten minutes on the doorstep. Can't she just wait in the car? And she seems to spend her whole time – trying to invite you to things. Like it's appropriate – every school event, every birthday party – really? I never get an invite. I wonder why I don't get a fucking invite?

Beat.

JOE. I'm not sure what we're talking about?

STEPH. I'm just saying – be wary.

JOE. Okay.

STEPH. Because you know – maybe – maybe she even has feelings for you.

JOE. She doesn't have feelings for me.

STEPH. I don't know –

JOE. The only feelings Anne has for me are irritation and –

STEPH. The way she was talking when I saw her – ?

JOE. Anne kicked me out.

STEPH. Why do you always say that?

JOE. – I just mean – she doesn't want me.

STEPH stares at him for a moment.

What?

STEPH. Nothing.

Beat.

Just good to – Sorry.

JOE. Okay.

STEPH continues collecting wood. She does this in total silence.

JOE watches.

Got some good pieces here. I'm going to teach you to start a fire using just a piece of flint and a rock. Find my kit. Come over here. You need to get close up.

She does so in silence.

So the key is to just strike the flint at an angle. Get a spark.

He tries.

Just got to catch it right.

He tries a few more times.

STEPH. Would you have left?

Beat.

You would have walked out? If it hadn't been her – you would of –

JOE. Steph.

STEPH. I'm just wondering –

JOE. – No.

STEPH. I just mean – I get it – you've got Ally –

JOE. Christ – Steph –

STEPH. I know.

JOE. This is what she does –

STEPH. You said –

JOE. Can't let her get to you.

STEPH. It's too late –

JOE. – What is?

STEPH. / I love you –

JOE. I love you too –

STEPH. Fuck. Joe. Fuck.

> *Pause.*

> It's like I knew – I mean you told me – I've met Ally – I've met your son – it's not like I didn't know.

> *Beat.*

> Remember that programme we were watching and that woman was trying to pump breast milk and it was squirting everywhere and you said 'That's nothing. Anne used to lie in a bath of milk, she had so much.' And we hadn't been seeing each other long so I tried to laugh it off. Pretend that I didn't now have an image burnt onto my mind of your ex in a bath of breast milk.

> But it's just seeing her –

JOE. – I don't?

> *This lingers.*

STEPH. When you came to see me at the clinic. I could feel it. With some people you just can – even before they tell you what is it – or lay down on the bed. I watched a man once – he was walking through town and I could see his aura – I actually saw it – black – like a big black mist following him.

Beat.

It was like that with you.

Beat.

But I just put my hands there. I just tried to move it – help it pass –

She's holding her hand up to JOE.

You told me that was because of Ally. It was losing him – you were afraid of losing him – ?

JOE. – Yeah.

STEPH *is looking at him closely.*

Of course.

She breaks the moment.

STEPH. Okay.

JOE. Are you – ?

STEPH. It's just me.

She tries to laugh it off.

Think I'm getting my period.

Beat.

JOE. Are you – ?

STEPH. Forget it. (*The flint.*) Let's get this fucker lit.

JOE *strikes it a few times – it lights and they rejoice – but there's something there now –*

JOE *paces*.

JOE. Okay – Okay, okay, okay.

There is something – it's something – because, I suppose,
yeah, I wanted to speak to you about this first. Because
I think it's important – that we talk about things. Talk things
through first. Because we're a team – You're my best pal.
I don't care what anyone says, you are. You're everything.
When I first held you, my whole world – I just played
Championship Manager all day. That's it. Then –

He does something that indicates an explosion.

That's you.

He does it again.

I had to grow up. I had to put you first.

Okay well –

Look. I'm trusting you. I'm treating you like a big boy. This
is between us. Just us. Between men. Grrrr. You understand?

He takes a breath.

I want to ask Steph to move in with us.

Because here's my thoughts – she's practically living here
already – isn't she? She's up in the morning. She's making
you breakfast. Playing Monopoly with you, when it's way
past your bedtime. You love having Steph here – and all this
means is she doesn't have to go home any more. She doesn't
need to cart her sad little memory-foam pillow back and
forth. I'm asking you because if you're not happy then I'm
not happy, but this would make me so, so – Ally, my nerves
are shot asking you because you say the word and it won't
happen. That's it. End of. But the thing is, since Steph came
into our lives things have been better.

So, what do you say?

What do you say?

ANNE *is tired, unpacking. Perhaps in her work uniform –*

ANNE. Back. *Back.* Brush them properly. *Properly.*

And pick up your cars. Keep still. Will you listen to me?
Alistair. *Alistair.* It's late. I've got a banging headache.
You've got school tomorrow – I've still got to do washing –

Did Daddy wash this?

She smells the clothes. Everything's washed and ironed.

And what about your script – where's your script?

She finds it.

Reads.

'Alistair knows all his lines.'

Pause.

Do you? You know all of them?

She takes out a piece of paper.

What's this? Homework? Alistair – What have I told you?
You need to tell your dad that you have homework. You need
to make sure – this is a whole volcano you've got to make by
tomorrow – how am I supposed to –

*She sees a plastic bag. She opens it up, pulls out a truly
amazing volcano.*

She stares at it for a long time. Then –

Did you make this?

No – it's –

And it erupts?

Wow. Wow-wee. That's – well that's just – I just hope it was
your thing. Your idea. I think it's important that you –

She can't breathe.

Create these things –

Evening. ANNE *hurries out into her garden. She silently
screams into a cushion.*

NEIGHBOUR. Is that you, Anne?

A NEIGHBOUR *leans over the fence. She's been smoking.*
ANNE *immediately composes herself.*

ANNE. Oh. Hi Helen. Didn't see you there.

NEIGHBOUR. Are you okay?

ANNE *tries to do something with the cushion.*

ANNE. Yeah. Great.

NEIGHBOUR. Just having a sneaky one, while Graham and the
  kids argue over what film to watch. It's the same every week.
  Everyone ends up watching something on a different device.

ANNE. Sounds fun.

NEIGHBOUR. Alistair's really growing up isn't he?

ANNE. He's eight now.

NEIGHBOUR. Heard him out here before. I was like 'Is that
  little Ally?'

ANNE. You didn't, did you? Oh God. I'm so sorry – he never
  swears. Never normally –

NEIGHBOUR. Oh – I didn't mean?

ANNE. Oh thought you meant – ?

NEIGHBOUR. No?

ANNE. Earlier. Had to tell him off. He's so good normally. He's
  just –

NEIGHBOUR. Pushing the boundaries?

ANNE. Joe just lets him watch whatever. Eat whatever. He's
  bouncing off the walls when he comes back. One of those
  days. Been counting the minutes till bedtime.

NEIGHBOUR. I hear you.

She reveals a bottle of wine behind the fence.

Want a glass?

ANNE. Yeah. Yeah I do, actually.

ANNE *runs inside to get a glass*. NEIGHBOUR *pours*.

NEIGHBOUR. They always try their luck when Daddy's gone – I mean, you know. Mine do when our Graham's away. Someone told me that apparently boys can't hear their mothers.

ANNE. What do you mean?

NEIGHBOUR. Well, they go through a stage of just tuning them out. Like they can only hear their fathers.

ANNE. That can't be true.

NEIGHBOUR. It's meant be like a primal thing. I saw Joe the other day actually.

ANNE. – Did you?

NEIGHBOUR. We were in Ikea. We've been in Ikea hell since we started that back bedroom.

ANNE. When?

NEIGHBOUR. Thursday night?

ANNE *thinks*.

ANNE. Thursday?

NEIGHBOUR. I think. Maybe –

The NEIGHBOUR *leans over the fence conspiratorially*.

I met her.

ANNE. Hm?

NEIGHBOUR. The 'girlfriend'.

Beat.

ANNE. Did you?

NEIGHBOUR. Do you like her?

ANNE. Don't really know her.

NEIGHBOUR. They were buying a new bed. Both lying on it, giggling.

ANNE. Right.

NEIGHBOUR. She asked this weird question.

ANNE. What?

NEIGHBOUR. Asked the sales assistant whether the mattress could be customised to hers and Joe's weight.

Beat.

Are you okay?

ANNE. Yeah.

NEIGHBOUR. I feel awful.

ANNE. Don't. Why?

NEIGHBOUR. It was bad enough – now they're living together?

ANNE. It's Alistair I'm worried about.

NEIGHBOUR. What does he think?

ANNE. She's going all out of whack – with the whole Disney stepmum thing. Like she's trying to prove something. But Alistair sees. Alistair knows.

NEIGHBOUR. Some people just can't be alone. They're actually in love with being in love. Remember how Joe used to leave you Post-It notes stuck to your windshield every morning? Just one of those types.

The NEIGHBOUR *is looking at her.*

I just want to say that you've handled this whole thing amazingly well.

ANNE. Thank you.

NEIGHBOUR. I don't know how you do it. I couldn't be a single mum. I really, really couldn't.

ANNE *drinks her wine.*

ANNE *feels it bubbling up for a moment –*

Suddenly sun, sea – she's closing her eyes breathing it in.

A beach.

She's running towards –

PETER, *a man in his early thirties, sat on a sun lounger facing out towards the sea, sunglasses on, headphones in. He's in good shape.*

She's smiling. She's soaking wet in her swimsuit. She shakes her towel out. PETER *reacts.*

PETER. Anne.

ANNE. Oh sorry!

PETER. I've just put suncream on.

ANNE. Sorry, babe.

PETER. It's everywhere.

    She tries to get rid of it.

ANNE. Freezing out there. We swam right out to that buoy – see the orange one? Were you watching?

PETER. It's all in my phone.

ANNE. You should go in. Alistair's a natural out there. He's like a little fish. (*Shouting.*) No. Stay where I can see you.

PETER. Are there jellyfish out there?

ANNE. It's just clear water the whole way.

PETER. I prefer the pool.

ANNE. You said you wanted to come to the beach.

PETER. Anything but watch lunchtime water aerobics.

ANNE. Your shoulder looks a bit red.

    ANNE *gets some suncream out and massages it into* PETER*'s shoulder.*

PETER. Ah. Now that is nice. I've got a knot there – will you dig in a bit. I'll have to go on a run tomorrow morning. Feel out a shape already.

ANNE. It's only been three days.

PETER. I've got Berlin in a month.

ANNE. I was thinking you should take Alistair.

PETER. To Berlin?

ANNE. On one of your little training runs. God knows he needs the exercise.

PETER. He couldn't keep up, Anne.

ANNE. You could train him. He sees you in all your running stuff. It's inspiring.

PETER. Yeah, maybe.

ANNE. Just round the block, see how he goes. (*Shouts.*) Alistair.

PETER. Just leave him for a minute.

ANNE. He needs a T-shirt on.

PETER. Can't we have two minutes?

ANNE *looks at* PETER. *Waves Alistair away.*

ANNE. That view. Look at him. I'm so glad we decided to do this. Sometimes you've just got to seize the moment – or whatever. Can't believe I almost didn't come. Almost let Joe ruin this.

PETER (*the suncream*). Rub some on my belly.

She does.

ANNE. It's been so good – just seeing you two together. I think it's brilliant how well you get along. You get on so well don't you?

PETER. – Yeah

ANNE. I mean what does Joe think – ? Anyway, I'm not even letting it get to me. I'm shaking it all off. I've left it all back there. Look at him. Look how bloody happy he is out there. Sun, sea – My two favourite boys. I'm going to frame that picture we took of us last night. I'm going to get it blown up – frame it. Joe still hasn't even put his collage up. Did I tell you?

I mean Alistair made it. All these pictures of him as
a baby. It's beautiful. She won't even let him hang it. It's
sitting in the bloody cupboard. How crazy is that?

PETER. Mad.

ANNE. And he has the cheek to talk to me? Joe won't even let
me knock on their front door now. He says 'park over the
road'. He comes running out. I said to Alistair last time, should
I honk my horn? Give it a big honk. 'Yooo-hooo I'm here.'

PETER (*the massage*). Not so hard –

ANNE. I mean he's missing out. That's the shame of it.
Sometimes Alistair does something brilliant – something
really funny – and I can't even share that with him any more –

PETER. Why would you want to?

ANNE. I don't. I'm just saying. We were amicable. Now this.

Beat.

You know, my mum – my mum she used to turn up in her
posh car. Dad never said anything. Never, nothing. Just 'Go
on now.' She'd take me out for the day. Look at my clothes
and say 'What has he been dressing you in?' She'd take me
shopping. Spend loads of money on all these new outfits for
me. Stuff I didn't even like. Wasn't me. How would she
know? Then – drop me back like a piece of luggage. I'd go
into my room – and I'd – I'd stuff them – stuff all those bags
to the back of my wardrobe. Shut the door. You mark my
words, sooner or later the kids find out.

PETER *suddenly pulls her on top of him.*

Peter!

PETER. What?

ANNE. Public beach.

PETER. Here.

He wraps a towel around her.

Is that better?

ANNE. Not really?

They kiss.

PETER. Now this is holiday.

ANNE. I just wanted to say –

He's trying to kiss her again.

Peter.

PETER. He can't see us.

ANNE. I know but –

PETER. Just a quick blowie.

ANNE. What?

PETER. Go under the towel.

ANNE. No –

PETER. Go on. Just for a laugh.

ANNE. *No.*

PETER *lifts her off him.*

He'll be in bed later.

PETER. Can we put him in Kids' Club tomorrow?

ANNE. He didn't like it.

PETER. He was only in it for half an hour.

ANNE. It's a windowless basement. Even the staff looked bored.

PETER. They have loads of stuff going on. I saw the timetable.

ANNE. It's just computers and TVs. He could get that home.

PETER. We booked this place because there was a Kids' Club –

ANNE. He said someone grabbed his arm.

PETER. No one grabbed his arm.

ANNE. There was a red mark.

PETER. He probably did it himself because he wants to spend every second of the day with you.

ANNE. Look, he's in the sea. He's not even bothering us.

Silence.

I just wanted to say about last night – what I said about these past few months – I've had so much fun. So good to remember this part of me. It's still here. And now, you're finally meeting Alistair –

PETER. Yeah.

ANNE. And I was thinking – about what you were saying too. And about how – yeah – maybe you're right. Maybe this is something we should work towards.

PETER. Towards?

ANNE. Like a little trial period?

PETER. A what – ?

ANNE. I mean, I want to do this right too. And God knows, I need help with the bills. You fork out so much on rent. Maybe it could work for both of us –

PETER. Whoa. What is this?

ANNE. Last night.

PETER. Yeah – ?

ANNE. When the ABBA tribute was on – We had a whole big discussion –

He looks at her blankly.

You said that we could test it out. You'd hold on to your place – but you would stay with us –

PETER. Move in?

ANNE. Just a couple of weeks at first –

PETER. No –

ANNE. A trial period – what you said –

PETER. No, no, no –

ANNE. Your idea Peter.

PETER. ABBA was on. I was fucked last night.

He's almost laughing.

Sorry. Sorry. But – what? Bloody hell Anne.

He's really laughing now.

Even this, even this has been a bit – much.

ANNE. What has?

PETER. This – all *this*. It's just all a bit claustrophobic – Okay?
He's jumping into our bed every morning. Twenty questions,
he's like a pair of clackers in my head. And he's always
climbing all over you.

ANNE. The heat's getting to you.

PETER. I'm a marathon runner I can handle the heat.

ANNE. Then maybe I'm getting to you.

PETER. Well yeah – *Moving in?*

He looks at her like she's mad.

Anne? Anne, come on? This is too, too much. I like you. I do
like you – but all this shit, shit with your ex? This isn't me
Anne. I have to be honest, don't I? Three-star all-inclusive,
bullshit. Everything is sticky in there – the bloody placemats
– everything.

Pause.

I'm sorry. I've been thinking that maybe it would be best if
we just – go back to how things were?

ANNE. How they were?

PETER. I like Al. But you've got so much going on right now.
And like you say – we were having fun. Proper fun together.
I'm just not looking for anything too – heavy.

ANNE. – Right.

PETER. You're great. You're such a great mum. You really are.
It just feels like that's what you want to focus on right now.

Beat.

We can still have a good time – can't we? Hey? Can't we?

ANNE. Yeah.

He gives her a squeeze.

PETER *puts his headphones in again, tinny music playing out.*

After a moment, she gets under the towel.

PETER. What are you doing?

PETER *is excited.*

Fucking hell, Anne.

He closes his eyes.

Suddenly his face changes.

Anne. (*Screams.*) Anne.

PETER *throws her off him.*

You fucking –

ANNE. Sorry.

He checks himself.

– Was an accident.

He stares at her.

JOE *and* STEPH *stand apart, in their living room.*

JOE. – I don't – how?

STEPH. The GP just said – nothing is a hundred per cent – or maybe it wasn't inserted properly –

JOE. Well that's not right –

STEPH. So the drug wasn't being released properly –

JOE. No – that's not right at all.

He paces for a moment, about to boil over.

No?

Beat.

No – that can't be right. I mean – fuck – ? What the fuck? You go to the NHS – the N – H – fucking – S. You trust them. You put your faith – They can't – they can't do this. This is negligence. This is negligence on a massive fucking scale –

STEPH. Joe?

JOE. Have you called them up? Have you told them what they've done?

STEPH. *Joe.*

Beat.

I'm – happy. Aren't you?

Pause.

JOE. You said – you had a what – it –

STEPH. I do.

JOE. A whatsit – in your arm –

STEPH. It's still in my arm –

JOE. You said that even without that it'd be a miracle –

STEPH. It is.

JOE. Your uterus thing – you've got the uterus thing –

STEPH. I know –

JOE. I just – I don't understand what's happening?

STEPH. It's just one of those things –

JOE. – One of those things? One of – ? I'm sorry – what? Like leaving the tea towel on the hob? Like missing the fucking post?

STEPH. Why are you swearing?

JOE. Because you said – You said this couldn't happen –

STEPH. It's amazing –

JOE. Amazing?

STEPH. You know – what I've been through. I'm nine weeks, Joe. *Nine*. I didn't even know. But there are all these stories out there now – on all these forums. It's not like when I was sixteen – the way they made it sound then. There are so many women out there – spent years trying – miscarriages – the lot – and then it's just happened. It's happened – at the right time for them.

JOE doesn't know where to put himself. He sits.

JOE. You should have been straight with me.

STEPH. About – ?

JOE. About this – about what you were planning.

STEPH. Planning?

JOE. Your implant – 'failed'?

STEPH. Excuse me? You think – ?

She stares him down.

JOE. No. No. I don't – Sorry. I'm sorry – just – *Fuck.*

He has his head in his hands.

STEPH. You're kind of ruining the –

He stays like that –

This is my moment too, Joe.

He stays.

Look I know – I know this is a shock. But – it's here. It's happening.

He looks at her.

You love me don't you – ?

JOE. Of course –

STEPH. Then it's not the end of the fucking world.

She goes to him.

Listen to me. I'm scared too – I'd made my peace with it – but I just have faith this time, Joe. I do. Because it's you and me. This is us. It's us this time –

JOE. What about Anne?

STEPH. – What?

JOE. I mean how she's going to –

STEPH. Anne?

JOE. I mean it's not like you're going to show – you probably won't show for a while yet. And maybe he'll be excited. Do you think? He used to ask for a little brother –– maybe we can get him excited –

STEPH. Joe.

She puts his hand to her stomach.

JOE. It's – too –

STEPH. Just –

He hesitates.

This. *This.*

She looks at him purposefully –

Okay?

She smiles at him – he tries.

ANNE *opens the suitcase – she brings out a T-shirt and holds it up – staring at it. She looks at Alistair.*

JOE *and* STEPH *are nervously/excitedly looking at Alistair too –*

ANNE. – What is this – ?

JOE. It's for you.

ANNE. This is new –

JOE. Can you read what it says?

ANNE. – 'I'm – going – to – be – a – big –

ALL. Big – brother.'

Pause.

JOE *and* STEPH *wait expectedly.*

JOE. – Well?

Beat.

Do you know what that means? / It means –

STEPH. It means –

JOE. No, you go on

STEPH. No – you –

JOE. You'll explain better –

STEPH. There's not much to – we're – 'we're'?

JOE. 'We're.' 'Us.'

STEPH. We're having a baby, Ally.

JOE. All of us.

They wait.

Argh – exciting. Are you excited?

STEPH. I'm not [showing] –

JOE. She's not fat yet –

He laughs, a little too much.

Can you believe it?

ANNE. Sorry – ?

JOE. Where's the scan – ?

STEPH. Oh it's –

JOE. Go get it.

STEPH. It's in my purse.

She hurries to fetch it.

JOE. We wanted to wait – We were going to take you along but then we thought just in case – I mean you never know – what these things pick up –

STEPH *is back.*

Here it is. Can you see? That's her head – her back –

STEPH. He keeps saying 'she' –

JOE. I don't know why I keep saying that.

STEPH. It's really early days – looks like a little peanut –

JOE. That's what we used to call you – 'Peanut'. We thought you were giving us the finger in yours. We did – you were like this – like this –

ANNE. – What is this – ?

STEPH. I'm fourteen weeks –

JOE. There's still a way to go –

STEPH. I'm due in January –

JOE. Could be an early Christmas present –

ANNE. / – I don't under–

JOE. Can I just say how happy I am – how proud. He's been brilliant – hasn't he?

ANNE. You knew – ?

STEPH. You're so grown up, Ally.

JOE. He's going to be the best, the bestest big brother

STEPH. It's a big change

ANNE. When?

JOE. / It's not going to change things –

ANNE. When did they give you this?

JOE. Nothing's going to change –

STEPH. I don't think we can say 'nothing'

JOE. Well there'll be a baby – of course they'll be a baby –

ANNE *is looking at Alistair – the utter betrayal – 'You didn't tell me – ?'*

It's just that – we'll be a family now. A real – a proper family.

ANNE *stares, slams the suitcase shut.*

Just JOE *and* ANNE.

ANNE – *deep-breathes, calming herself down.*

JOE *opens the suitcase.*

JOE *takes a piece of paper out of the case – reads –*

JOE. Banana: High in potassium, contains histamine-lowering nutrients, magnesium and vitamin C. What's this?

ANNE. Alistair's eczemas flares up when he's – he's – stressed. He's had it really bad over the last couple weeks – after *everything.*

JOE (*a roll of the eyes*). 'Everything.'

ANNE. We've been following this diet. He *needs* to stick to it.

JOE. Beef or chicken broth: Provides skin-repairing amino acid glycine.

Potato: Rich in fibre, potassium, vitamin C and is alkalising. Green onions: What are green onions?

ANNE. Contain histamine-lowering, anti-inflammatory quercetin and rich source of vitamin K, important for healthy skin.

JOE. Buckwheat? Buck – wheat?

ANNE. Gluten-free and contains quercetin to lower histamine and has strong anti-inflammatory effect –

JOE. Rice milk. Fuck off. Sorry –

ANNE. Low-allergy and low in chemicals and considered eczema-safe –

Mung-bean sprout –

JOE. Mung-bean sprouts?

He tears up the paper.

I'm sorry.

ANNE. Strong alkalising foods –

JOE. If your mum wants to do all this stuff with you, fine. But actually, I don't have buckwheat and mung beans in right now. Your eczema isn't even that bad –

ANNE. Your dad hasn't seen you scratching with a hairbrush till it bleeds.

JOE. I had eczema when I was a child. I grew out of it.

ANNE. I'm the one, smothering you in emollient. Googling treatments till the early hours –

JOE. Anyway – forget it.

ANNE. Keeping the house totally dust-free. Taking you back and forth to see the dermatologist –

JOE. Weekends are supposed to be about treats.

ANNE. What did you eat?

JOE. When you're at my house you can eat what I give you. When you're at your mum's –

ANNE. Dairy? *Dairy?* Alistair – your arms are red raw.

Christ.

I'll make the meals. I'll label them and put them in containers for when you go to your dad's.

JOE *takes out a container. Smells it and squirms.*

JOE. You eat this?

ANNE. Promise me you'll eat this.

JOE *laughs.*

JOE. What is she doing to you?

ANNE. Did you eat it?

JOE. Jesus Christ.

ANNE. Did Daddy give it to you? Tell the truth.

JOE. We'll just –

He puts it in the bin.

We'll just tell your mum, you had some.

ANNE. Some?

JOE. Just tell her it was yummy.

Go on.

It's fine.

ANNE. Did you eat it Alistair or not?

Did you even try it?

Did you?

JOE *is chuckling to himself.*

I don't understand –

Look at your skin –

JOE. Your skin is fine. You're bloody fine –

ANNE. *You're not fine* –

This is what happens –

This is the result –

JOE. Just put that food away /

ANNE. Not even a taste?

Nothing?

JOE. There's nothing to worry about –

ANNE. Blood on your sheets –

JOE. Just chill out will you?

ANNE. Scratching, scratching –

JOE. *Ally.* Just leave it.

JOE *has a box of takeaway pizza.*

You're saying you don't want this?

ANNE. Don't you dare –

JOE. Meat feast – stuffed crust –

ANNE. Don't you –

JOE. Gooey – mozzarella?

ANNE. *Alistair* –

JOE. Come on –

> ANNE *hits it out of* JOE*'s hand.*

ANNE. *No.*

> *Beat.*

> The time I've spent – making – for you – this is for you. Because it's good – Because it's what you need – And you just want to throw it – ? Chuck it in the bin? Like it, means – like it means – like it means –

> ANNE *is trying not to cry.*

JOE. Ally.

> JOE *chuckling in disbelief.*

> It's just pizza.

A short flight away – Ireland or Guernsey.

ALAN *and* JOE *on a boat. The cold of an early morning.*

Silence.

JOE *drinks from a beer can.* ALAN *watches.*

ALAN *feels a pull on his line.*

ALAN. Oh. Ey up. Ey up son. Grab the line.

JOE. What? No.

ALAN. Come on. It's for you.

JOE. I don't want it.

ALAN. Have a go.

JOE. No.

ALAN. Come on. Oh shit. It's a big one.

JOE *gets up*.

Don't get up. Grab the line.

JOE. I don't want to.

ALAN. Help me reel it in.

ALAN *reels the line in*.

On the end is a fish skeleton. He flicks it towards JOE, *and almost sends him flying out the boat*.

JOE. – What are you doing?

ALAN *laughs*.

ALAN. It's just a –

JOE. What the fuck?

ALAN. It's just a fish skeleton.

JOE. I nearly fell out.

He wipes some beer off his jacket.

ALAN. I hooked it onto the line when you were getting your coat on. Your face.

JOE. Great.

ALAN. It was a joke.

JOE. Fun.

ALAN. Remember how scared you used to be of fish skeletons? Chasing you round the house with one?

JOE. I still don't like them.

ALAN. That's what I thought.

JOE. No, I *really* don't.

ALAN. You still know how to sulk. Don't you?

ALAN *tries to tease him with the fish skeleton*.

It doesn't work.

Just enjoying you.

ALAN *gets his flask and pours some green liquid into the lid. Knocks in back. Shudders.*

Wheatgrass. All your veg and goodness for the day. Part of my new regime. Want to try some?

JOE *shakes his head.*

ALAN *drinks it. Makes a show of how good it is for him.*

Hey?

JOE. It's good you're getting – right.

ALAN. Have to. Have to my son. No choice. I've got a scar from there to there. Do you wanna see?

JOE. S'alright.

ALAN. Touch-and-go it was. Jan lit a candle. She's my rock she is. Thank God for her.

Pause.

You look like Alistair. That look. I was on whatsit? Skype to him the other night. I was thinking, it's like stepping back in time. He sends me postcards you know.

JOE. I saw.

ALAN. Did you? Lovely that. No one send postcards these days.

JOE *is looking at* ALAN.

JOE. Yeah. Look. I wanted to talk to you –

ALAN. Hm?

JOE. I wanted to say, about that. You can call him when he's with me you know?

ALAN. Oh right.

JOE. I can get him to call you.

ALAN. That would be nice.

JOE. You don't have to call Anne.

ALAN. – She calls me.

JOE. Well either way. I'd prefer it if you weren't in touch with her from now on – with everything that's going on.

Pause.

Can you do that?

ALAN. Well. I don't know.

JOE. Just talk to him through me. That's all I'm asking. I can Skype.

ALAN. I know but –

JOE. I'm not asking much.

ALAN. I can't just – not pick up the phone to her. Can I?

JOE. Just phase her out.

ALAN. She calls me up.

JOE. I'll call you up.

ALAN. You don't call.

JOE. I'm asking you.

Beat.

I've never asked you for anything.

ALAN. Whoa.

JOE. I wouldn't if it wasn't –

ALAN. Where has this come from?

JOE. It's important to me.

ALAN. Don't be silly.

ALAN *wheezes, searches for his bag.*

JOE. I am just asking you –

ALAN. Or what?

JOE. I don't want to argue.

ALAN *finds an inhaler. A couple of intakes.*

Don't get wound up –

He holds his chest.

Are you all right?

ALAN. Yeah – Just sometimes.

ALAN *breathes for a few moments.*

You know me. I won't be told. My home, Joe. Okay?

Pause.

JOE. Are you loaning her money?

Pause.

Dad. Are you loaning her money?

ALAN. No –

JOE. Are you?

ALAN. I can't have stress. Do you understand?

JOE. I'm just asking a question.

ALAN. The doctor has told me –

JOE. It's a simple question.

ALAN. Where is this coming from?

JOE. I know you're loaning her money.

ALAN. We're supposed to be out here – having a fish. Nice little time together. Come on.

ALAN *shifts about awkwardly.*

I mean. Christ. I'm not loaning her money. I've given her little bits. Money for Alistair.

JOE. I provide money –

ALAN. Well she says – You're not.

JOE *holds it in.*

JOE. She's using you –

ALAN. She wants to come and see me. She wants to bring Alistair out here – Actually.

JOE *laughs*.

JOE. And you think that's going to happen?

ALAN. She's been looking at flights.

JOE. She doesn't –

ALAN. You shouldn't talk to me this way. I invite you out here – nice little break. Jan's been cooking for you –

JOE. I haven't seen him in four weeks. Okay?

Beat.

Oh she didn't mention that did she? She left that bit out did she? I have to wait until the – the fucking court hearing.

ALAN. Court?

JOE. So I can get a piece of paper – that says the days – that says the times. So she can stop messing me about. Picking him up from school before I get there. Being out when I'm supposed to pick him up. Constantly cancelling, fucking up my plans. It wasn't so long ago that she took him off on holiday with some total dickhead she'd been seeing just a few months. Now she won't even answer my calls. She says that if I want to take her to court, then I'll have to wait till then to see him. But if I stop her money – if I stop the direct debit, Dad. That's my only card – I say fine. You wanna stop me seeing him then you're not getting shit from me, either. But that's only going to work – it only works if you're not giving her anything –

ALAN. I don't know –

JOE. You don't know – what?

ALAN. I don't like to get involved –

JOE. You're involved – You've involved yourself –

ALAN. I don't think it's right – If you want to know the truth. She's the mother of your kid. There's a way to behave.

JOE. You're telling me – ?

ALAN. I never messed your mum about over money.

JOE. You didn't give her any.

ALAN. Gave her the house.

JOE. She had to work three jobs.

ALAN. You have no idea –

> JOE *stands up in the boat.*

> Steady.

> *A moment.*

> JOE *sits.*

> Where's this come from ey? We're having a nice time. Why can't we have a nice time?

JOE. When I drop Ally off. He won't even wave to me if his mum's there. I try to talk to him – I try – She isn't going to do this. She isn't going to fuck up my relationship with him.

> *Beat.*

> I want shared custody. I want this all straightened out before the baby comes. It's important for kids to have consistency. Me and Steph both believe – it's about structure – this is damaging him – *she's* damaging him – out of spite. Pure spite. Just because I'm finally getting my life back.

> *Beat.*

> This is the longest I've gone without seeing him.

> *Beat.*

ALAN. Is this why you're here?

> *Beat.*

> Christ. Joe. I'm thinking – finally – he comes.

JOE. I just need to be able to cut her money –

ALAN. Joe –

JOE. These people from the courts, they're going to ask what he wants –

ALAN. Joe – listen to me.

JOE. It's all about 'access' – 'contact' – I'm his fucking father –

ALAN. *Joe*.

JOE *looks at him*.

It's not good. Not good to have all this inside you. Do you
know what I'm saying? Not good. You've got to forgive.
You've got to – put past behind you – find it in your heart. If
I could go back – if I could live it again. I'd make peace with
your mother – I'd make peace with her –

JOE. I don't want –

ALAN. We've got to be kind to each other, We've to find it in
our hearts – if your mum was here, I would. I'd do it a
hundred times over –

JOE. *You'd* forgive – ?

ALAN. I'd make peace –

JOE. Because last time I checked –

ALAN. You're going to spend your life locked in this. Do you
hear me? You're going to waste it all – with this – this thing
you're carrying – Till it balls up, till it becomes so tight and
heavy – so tight –

He indicates – his heart.

Doctor said it's a miracle I'm still ticking over.

Beat.

You've got to forgive. Forgive, Joe.

JOE *stares at him*.

JOE. The last time me and Anne argued – we'd been out. We're
in our kitchen. I'm a piss-poor everything – biggest mistake
of her life. Shit in bed. Shit at everything. Her and Alistair
would be better off. Going and going and going –

Beat.

Punched my hand through the door panel. I wasn't – wasn't
aiming at her – but I was thinking about her.

Beat.

ALAN. You're not me.

Beat.

I'm not even that 'me' any more.

JOE *looks at his father.*

JOE. I need distance. I need a piece of paper and distance –

ALAN. Joe –

JOE. Just – stop the money. That's all.

ALAN *hesitates* –

He tries to drink some more wheatgrass.

Gives up and tosses it.

ANNE *is frantically tidying round her kitchen. Putting flowers in a vase. She takes it all in. Fixes herself. Takes a breath* –

The CAFCASS WORKER *sat opposite* ANNE *making notes as* ANNE *talks.*

ANNE. I have tried – I have gone out of my way. Invited him round here on numerous occasions – sit down, talk things through with me and Alistair – he refuses. He refuses to believe that any of this is actually real. Made a whole show of himself in front of the judge. Trying to make out that *I'm* the baddie. That *I'm* the bad guy here? Alistair is a very bright – articulate young boy. He knows his own mind. He knows his own feelings. He just wants his dad to listen –

CAFCASS. Uh-huh.

ANNE. I mean it's bad enough that I have to send my child off to a place where I know he's not happy – but then I can't even contact him whilst he's there? Joe won't even let him speak to me – not even at bedtime – ?

CAFCASS. I see.

ANNE. This is what Joe does. Buries his head. Alistair comes home – he's clinging to me. Following me from room to room. And then I find out that they've sent him to bed early again. Joe doesn't even get up for breakfast any more. Just lays around in bed with her all morning. And then she's telling Alistair to be quiet. That Sunday mornings are 'quiet time'. I told him that that was his dad's house before it was hers and he can make as much noise as he bloody well wants.

The CAFCASS OFFICER *looks at* ANNE *before writing something more.* ANNE *fears she hasn't said the right thing.*

He was even threatening to cut my money'.

CAFCASS. Do you prevent him from seeing Alistair?

ANNE. Only when Alistair is refusing to go. The other week, I sent him, he comes back, full of anger. Finally, he bursts into tears. He tells me that he locked himself in the bathroom at their house. Apparently, Steph had been having a clear-out – making room, making room for the new baby it seems. She was chucking his stuff in bin bags. She chucked his old teddy bear. She said it looked like a matted hairbrush and how was she supposed to know? She knew. She knew all right. And what did Joe do? Joe made Alistair apologise – to Steph. *To her.*

She stares incredulous.

That teddy bear – That teddy – when he was in the special care baby unit – I didn't want to leave his side. Hated even going for a shower. I asked his dad to go to the little hospital shop to get something. Joe comes back with this bright pink teddy. 'Pinky.' I laughed. The only one they had left. First night I slept with it, close to my neck. One of the nurses said – No perfume, no fragrances, but just sleep with it close to you. So that it smells of you, and then place it in there with him. It'll soothe him. It'll help him sleep. And it did. It did.

Beat.

And she just threw it away? *He just let her?*

CAFCASS. Prior to these issues, Joe was having Alistair one overnight during the week and two overnights every other weekend – is that right?

ANNE. – I think so –

CAFCASS. And what he is now proposing is that there would be a better continuity of care for Alistair if you had shared residency – a fifty-fifty split.

ANNE. No –

CAFCASS. Fifty-fifty is just a fair starting point. Joe has put forward that he would be happy for three overnights to your four each week –

ANNE. No, sorry. I'm sorry – ? Have you been listening – ?

CAFCASS. Anne, there has not been any legitimate reason put forward so far, to not have a child arrangement order that reflects shared care –

ANNE. I've been telling you –

CAFCASS. Joe lives locally. He is able to arrange pick-up and drop-offs at school for the days that he has Alistair –

ANNE. You mean Steph? He'll be asking Steph?

CAFCASS. Anne –

ANNE. You haven't even spoken to my son yet –

CAFCASS. I will be –

ANNE. His wishes and feelings, they told me –

CAFCASS. His thoughts are taken into account but they're not the deciding factor. You should start to think about how you would like this to work – the days that work best for you. Holidays. Christmas is coming. You might want to think about how you split that day.

ANNE. Split it?

CAFCASS. Joe has him in the morning, you in the afternoon or vice versa –

ANNE. Alistair is refusing to go there –

CAFCASS. Joe is a good father. You said so yourself.

ANNE. Did I?

CAFCASS. In your first statement.

ANNE. You haven't seen the text messages. The way he speaks to me. It's both of them. I'm 'damaging' my son? *Me?* She has the *gall?* Well I'm sorry love. But you don't know what it takes – what I do for him morning till night. You haven't the first bloody clue. I am the only one fighting his corner. My son tells me that he has to sit on the floor while they're curled up on the sofa together. He lies awake wishing he could call me but he's too scared to ask because my name is black – is mud there. And now even you –

ANNE *can't speak. The* CAFCASS OFFICER *is getting her things together.*

CAFCASS. We can make a stipulation in the order that Joe is to get Alistair to call you when he's in his care. But my recommendation stands – a shared residency would be in Alistair's best interests.

ANNE. That's it? He's not safe –

CAFCASS (*firmly*). All the safeguarding checks have been done, Anne.

ANNE *is panicking.*

So if there's nothing else – ?

ANNE *pours a large wine –*

ANNE. I have to laugh. I have to laugh or I'll – I'm sorry. I'm so sorry. I don't want you to see me like this. *Christ.*

She's trying to calm herself.

You know what really gets me? About all of this? Do you know?

JOE *is clicking his fingers.*

JOE. Ally –

ANNE. – Adamant – so bloody adamant. I did everything, everything I could – persuade him, make him see.

JOE. Just focus – focus on me for a minute, Ally –

ANNE. I always thought eventually he'd come around –

JOE. This is important –

ANNE. All I ever wanted – He knew that. He knew what it meant –

JOE. Because maybe I haven't? I haven't been spending enough time – is that it?

ANNE. He never budged.

JOE. Is that it Ally?

ANNE. Never – never – Not for a moment. He thought I could just come to terms with it. Just accept it.

JOE. I miss us. We're missing out on so much.

ANNE. We were happy with you and that was it.

JOE. Morning cuddles. Your little cold feet in the morning –

ANNE. And of course, we were darling – we were –

JOE. But we're going to get it all back – I swear to you –

ANNE. But – every time I watched you playing on your own? Watched all the little brothers and sisters at the school gates?

JOE. I've never said a bad word against your mum.

ANNE. I couldn't help but think – we should have this. We should have had it.

JOE. But –

ANNE. Instead he's –

JOE. *But* –

ANNE. *Punishing me* –

JOE. You know it.

ANNE. This is all to punish –

JOE. You know what she's like –

ANNE. Fuck him.

JOE. You know what she does. You do.

ANNE. I'm sorry. I'm sorry.

JOE. But we're not going to let her are we? Our time is going to be our time again –

ANNE. I never swear. You know me. This isn't me.

JOE. I just need you on my side. I need you to tell them –

ANNE. You have to tell them. You have to make them understand, Alistair.

JOE. You get on with Steph. You love Steph. All the days out. All the things we used to do together?

ANNE. She wouldn't even let you go in the cupboards for a biscuit – remember? Remember that?

JOE. You were excited about the baby –

ANNE. These are the things.

JOE. Until *she* –

ANNE. Oh God.

JOE. *She* –

ANNE. Why fight it?

JOE. Twists things. She has a way –

ANNE. Why am I even trying?

JOE. You have to see through it, Ally. You have to be strong.

ANNE *is upset.*

ANNE. I never thought –

JOE. I'm hurting too –

ANNE. Never thought –

JOE. I need you too –

ANNE. This would be us.

ANNE *in bed.*

She is sleeping in. She has been like this for days.

ANNE *slowly wakes up to find a little tray left on her bed. Alistair has made her breakfast. There's a little flower and a handmade card left for her. She opens it and reads – it means everything to her.*

ANNE *– tired-looking – composing herself – is on the phone –*

ANNE. – There is something.

She hesitates.

I – I – didn't say before – I didn't want to. I didn't think it would come to this but – it's something you should know.

Joe – Joe had a breakdown. It was – what do they call it? PTSD – post-traumatic – It was a couple of months after Alistair was born. Joe was having night terrors. He became quite neurotic. Collecting things – in the garage. Stuff we didn't even need. Like toilet paper – protein bars. He'd just watch the news all day. And go on runs. He kept disappearing on these big long runs. He cried during a meeting at work. They signed him off. He was put on anti-depressants – I can't remember which. This will all be in his doctor's notes – won't it? One night he was having one of his nightmares – he elbowed me in the face. I had to go to the emergency dentist. I can probably find something on that too.

Beat.

They referred him to a sleep clinic, they thought that maybe – maybe the root of all this was the birth. I had quite a traumatic – maybe that was the trigger.

The way he's been acting lately – I'm sure you understand. My priority has to be my son.

Banging. The middle of the night.

JOE *putting up shelves. His hand is wrapped in bloody tissue. There's a few empty beers on the side.* STEPH *appears – half-asleep, dazed. She's in later pregnancy.*

STEPH. What are you doing?

He hasn't seen her.

  Joe.

JOE. What are you doing up?

STEPH. What time is it?

JOE. You shouldn't be up.

STEPH. I heard a yell.

JOE. You need your rest. Go on. Get back to bed.

STEPH. What's going on?

JOE. Just sorting out the garage.

STEPH. Now?

JOE. You said, we need a clear-out.

STEPH. You've got work in the morning.

JOE. No use tossing and turning.

STEPH. Come back to bed.

JOE. You said – you wanted me to sort shit out around the house.

STEPH. What's happened to your hand?

  STEPH *goes to look.*

JOE. It's nothing.

STEPH. Let me see.

JOE. It's fine.

He carries on banging.

STEPH. Joe.

He isn't listening.

  Joe.

JOE. What?

She stares at him.

I'm fine. I'm just getting stuff out the way. We need shelves. We need proper storage. I can't move in here for all the crap. You're right; we need a proper declutter before Christmas – before the baby.

STEPH. Is this about the letter?

Beat.

Is this about Ally?

JOE. I'm not thinking about that –

STEPH. Good because we said –

JOE. I don't want you worrying.

STEPH. I need to know that you're okay –

JOE. I'm okay.

STEPH. Because you need to step away from this – as difficult as it is –

JOE. Steph – I don't need –

STEPH. It isn't good for you, Joe. You need to just accept what the report says.

Beat.

JOE. Just accept – ?

STEPH. For now –

JOE. Accept it?

STEPH. You said –

JOE. One Saturday – in every fourteen – ?

STEPH. The court always goes with their recommendations –

JOE. That woman was a fucking snake –

STEPH. She was just doing her job –

JOE. That report is full of lies –

STEPH. It's a just a temporary solution –

JOE. Anne's mother of the fucking year?

STEPH. It's what Ally wants.

JOE. That's not him –

STEPH. They interviewed him –

JOE. With his mum's ear pressed to the wall.

STEPH. We just need a breather don't we? All this? Sometimes it's best to just give things time –

JOE. Time?

STEPH. Let things settle –

JOE. The more he's with her –

STEPH. Just for a little bit –

JOE. The worse things get – bitch.

He continues banging.

Bitch.

STEPH. Joe. I can't have this around me any more. I'm sorry. It isn't good for either of us. I've been thinking – You know – maybe now. Maybe it's time to look at it. Moving closer to my parents. We'll have some support – *Joe.*

JOE. What?

STEPH. The schools are so good –

JOE. What are you talking about?

STEPH. We've talked about it –

JOE. I'm not moving.

STEPH. Don't I get a say?

JOE. You want me to move even further – ?

STEPH. It's half an hour –

JOE. How is that going to look –?

STEPH. To who?

JOE. When we appeal this –

STEPH. You get Saturdays.

JOE. Are you – pleased?

Beat.

STEPH. What?

JOE. You didn't help.

STEPH. – Help?

JOE. You didn't help clean the house.

STEPH. – Sorry?

JOE. Before the Cafcass worker arrived – You didn't help tidy
up. It was all me –

STEPH. I got out of the house –

JOE. Exactly, you left.

STEPH. She wasn't here to talk to me.

JOE. Do you not think it would have looked good – if you were
there? Supporting me?

STEPH. You think this is because of me – ? This is nothing to
do with me. Any of this.

JOE *pulls the crumpled-up report out of his pocket.*

JOE. He doesn't feel like it's 'his home any more'.

STEPH. Why have you – ?

JOE. He doesn't think that he's wanted here.

STEPH. And that's my –

JOE. You never hug him.

STEPH. What?

JOE. I've never seen it.

STEPH. I bake cakes – I help him with his maths. I watch shit
TV with him – let him eat a whole giant Toblerone in his bed.
Before he came back, I tidied out his whole room. New
bedsheets. Action figures in a line. He loved it. But what
comes back? I accidentally threw out some stupid teddy bear?

Some old scraggly thing that looked like it had been won on a grabbing machine. That's what he remembers. That's the only thing –

JOE. You made a big deal about his Lego being in our room.

STEPH. Because he has a room –

JOE. In our bed –

STEPH. I'm not even allowed – ?

JOE. Like it matters – like it was a big thing –

STEPH. His shit is everywhere –

JOE. This is his house too –

STEPH. That is my bed –

JOE. It was just some fucking Lego –

STEPH. The bath is surrounded with bath toys. Boxes of toys in the living room. The hallway has his bike – his scooter – his own room is overflowing. Can't I have one place in this whole house that I don't have to share? That is just ours. Just fucking mine and yours?

Pause.

All those things she said Joe? All those things she told them? I mean Christ you even had to have a hair-strand test because she said Ally had seen you drinking a lot. And when they were asking you about this baby – about how you're handling this pregnancy – how you feel about this – whether you're going to cope – They could have referred us on to Social Services –

JOE. That wouldn't have happened –

STEPH. I have to protect us, Joe. Someone has to –

JOE. You need some rest.

STEPH. I need you –

JOE. You need sleep

STEPH. I take myself off. I light candles. But I just feel blocked. I can feel it. Here. Trapped. All this. Bad energy

building up – me you, Ally – *her*. And there's a line between
this baby and me – so it's all going to there – And I can't
stop it. It's completely out of my control –

JOE. I'm sorry.

STEPH. We need you –

JOE. / I shouldn't be bringing you into this.

STEPH. *We* do –

JOE. I'm going to sort it –

He hammers.

STEPH. Joe?

Hammers. Harder, harder.

JOE.

Windy.

JOE *is changing into his outdoor gear, backpack. During the
following he starts to run.*

ANNE – *sticking a 'Sold' sign back into the ground.*

The NEIGHBOUR *appears watching.*

NEIGHBOUR. Are you okay?

ANNE doesn't hear her.

Are you okay?

She sees her.

ANNE. These winds.

NEIGHBOUR. You can just get up and go. Amazing. What'll
you do?

ANNE. When?

NEIGHBOUR. When you get there?

ANNE. We're staying with my dad for a bit. He's talked about converting the garage at the bottom of his garden into an apartment for me and Alistair.

NEIGHBOUR. A garage?

ANNE. I know how that sounds, but it's huge. Honestly. Two floors – him and Trish in the big house, me and Alistair in our own little maisonette.

NEIGHBOUR. Sounds – wow.

ANNE. It's a beautiful place –

NEIGHBOUR. Saw Steph.

Beat.

Just through the Christmas rush, shopping.

Beat.

She's getting big. Ally's going to be a big brother.

ANNE. Alistair.

NEIGHBOUR. What?

ANNE. / It's always been Alistair.

NEIGHBOUR. What does Joe think?

ANNE. About what?

NEIGHBOUR. About – You. Moving.

ANNE. He can't stop us.

NEIGHBOUR. You're going so far –

ANNE. I'm doing it for Alistair.

NEIGHBOUR. / Surely this is a bit –

ANNE. You know what, Helen.

She takes a breath.

I get it. I do. You have your husband and your kids. There's no better feeling than walking through Tesco with your little tribe. But you get scared. You get scared when you look at me because you know – one day. Probably. You're me.

But you don't have to be afraid, Helen. I'm telling you. I'm
great. I'm just fine thank you. For the first time in my life
I am proud – I have had to rely on myself for everything –
And I know now – I can do it – I can –

She stabs the sign into the ground.

I am Alistair's mum.

Trust that.

No better compass than that.

This is the one thing that is good and true.

Completely fucking unshakable –

JOE *batting down his shelter in the woods.*

ANNE *has forced her way into* JOE *and* STEPH*'s home,
searching, frantically.*

JOE. Here we are – base camp. This is base camp son. You've
got to imagine this – No water. No electricity. No kitchen.
Completely 'OTG'. That's 'Off The Grid'. We've got a lake.
We've got sleeping bags. It's going to be up to us Ally.

STEPH. / You can't just barge in, here – Anne – *Anne* –

ANNE. *Where are they?*

JOE. We're going to be the protectors of the camp. We're going
to make our own weapons. Knife skills. Axe throwing.
Important to have a variety of hunting tools

ANNE. Joe picked Alistair up from school –

STEPH. He's not here –

ANNE. Where are they? Where's Joe?

JOE. – Ally. Ally. Focus – come on. Outside is ending. Floods,
fires, droughts and storms. Nothing on the shelves, in the
banks, in the petrol stations.

ANNE. His phone's switched off –

JOE. Maybe it's engineered diseases, nuclear war.

ANNE. It's getting dark –

JOE. There's a solar flare exploding in the sky.

ANNE. He's taken him –

STEPH. He'll be okay –

ANNE. You know that?

JOE. But I've got you and you've got me.

ANNE. / Oh God –

JOE. Look at us –we're ready.

Later – just JOE *in the woods – cooking on the fire. It's cold.*

You've got to appreciate these times, you know? Look around. Breathe it in. I just love this – connection. Trees, birds. I used to come here – after me and your mum split. I'd spend five days or more. The longer I was here – the more I'd feel – camping under the stars – it was all going to be okay. This is it – this is all –

Ally – don't.

This is all /

Don't mess with that.

I'm just trying to say – Giving yourself time – Connecting to that deeper part – that part of you /

It's not cold. It's not –

That knows – everything going to be okay. Hey? You know that – ? Ally? Ally. Just look at me. Come on. I'm just trying to share – I'm trying to say –

He gives up.

Brought some old photographs.

He's showing Alistair pictures.

Here – me and you – see?

Sand dunes. Chips and gravy – remember that?

Beautiful day. The Pierhead.

Are you looking? You're not looking. Ally. You need to look properly. Christ. My dad? He'd take me to the pub. Leave me in the car, push three bags of Frazzles through the window. Do you know how lucky you are? All this. You've got to appreciate –

We went on one of the ships. Remember? You must remember that. Hey? Hey? What's wrong with you?

ANNE *and* STEPH *are flashes of memory.*

ANNE. There are things going on right now, Alistair.

JOE. What's the matter?

ANNE. Things that I can't tell you about.

JOE. You're not being fair to me here. I bring you out here. This is supposed to be a nice time –

ANNE. I need you on my side –

JOE. Aren't you having a good time?

STEPH. It really early days –

JOE. Throw this picture in the fire – would that bother you?

STEPH. Looks like a little peanut, doesn't it?

JOE. I just need something here. I need something back –

ANNE. Look after him, keep him safe okay?

STEPH. It looks like a matted hairbrush.

JOE (*the photos*). This is me, this is us.

ANNE. You have to tell them. You have to make them understand, Alistair –

STEPH. You're so grown up Ally.

JOE. Are you even listening?

STEPH. It's a big change.

JOE. Do you want to go home – is that it?

ANNE. Where's my brave boy when I need him?

JOE. Do you actually want to leave? Because that'll be it for us Ally.

ANNE. We were happy –

JOE. That'll be it.

ANNE. When you were born –

JOE. Your mum's taking you away.

ANNE. They said – they told me –

JOE. You know that? You understand?

ANNE. Excruciating, cut me twice –

JOE. Do you actually want to go?

STEPH. His shit is everywhere –

ANNE. Give me my baby –

STEPH. Everywhere –

JOE. Ally.

ANNE. Alistair –

JOE. Ally –

ANNE. Alistair –

JOE. *Ally* –

ANNE *slowly opens the suitcase. Put things in.*

ANNE. – And there's a Christmas tree up to the ceiling.
Granddad says he's been waiting for you to put the star on
top. Just you wait – It even smells better there, Alistair.

Beat.

You know, this is the only thing, I've ever done well – being
your mum. Walk through hot coals. Cut my right arm off –
I have to trust –

Beat.

I know, know what it's like, Alistair. I went to stay with my
mum once. I went to meet them. I felt like a visitor. I was a
visitor. This was their mother now. *Their* mother. I had to
sleep on a mattress on the floor. All these photographs round
the house. One of those studio portraits of all of them, pride
of place. Could feel the relief of everyone when it was over –
ushering me back out the door. My mum holding her new
baby. With her 'See you soon. Don't be a stranger.' Who says
that? Who says that to a child? And I'm packed off home to
my dad. Just me and him. He's snoring in his chair. Bin piled
high – and I don't want you to feel – What I felt. Do you
understand? Because it's never the same. Nothing is ever the
same again – as must as people try. Like a cut that can't heal.
You've just got to rip the Band-Aid off. Just rip it.

Night. A layby. JOE *is in a car. A* POLICEMAN *is
breathalysing him through the window.*

JOE *tries to blow into the machine.*

POLICEMAN. Wait till the light goes off.

He tries again.

Till the light goes off. Thirty seconds.

He tries again.

It'll make a beep. That wasn't long enough.

JOE. I'm sorry.

POLICEMAN. Try again.

JOE. Don't know what's wrong with me.

POLICEMAN. Take your time.

> JOE *tries again. This time he gets it.*
>
> *The* POLICEMAN *looks at it.*

You're borderline.

JOE. Really?

POLICEMAN. You're just within the limit.

JOE. Wow. I hadn't –

POLICEMAN. Any more and you'd be over.

JOE. I didn't realise. I really, I didn't.

POLICEMAN. Even in a parked car, that would be it.

JOE. I know.

POLICEMAN. Not a great start to the new year is it?

JOE. No.

POLICEMAN. What are your plans for tonight?

JOE. Just sitting in. Jools Holland, probably.

POLICEMAN. How far to your girlfriend's?

JOE. Not far. Like, less than half an hour.

POLICEMAN. Drive safely.

JOE. It won't happen again.

> *Pause.*

POLICEMAN. If you were thinking of sleeping here, it's not safe. A lot of lorries driving past here. It's not well lit. I'd pull into a service station.

JOE. Okay.

POLICEMAN. I'm going to drive past here again in an hour and I want to see this car gone.

POLICEMAN *goes to walk away, then comes back.*

If you do need somewhere to stay overnight, there's a campsite just down the road on the right. A lot safer. Electric hook-up. Showers. Tenner a night. I've been with the kids. Lovely place.

JOE *cries for the first time.*

– Are you really okay?

JOE. Yes.

POLICEMAN. I don't have a tissue.

JOE. Fuck.

POLICEMAN. It's all right –

JOE. Sorry.

POLICEMAN. You should call a friend.

JOE. I know.

POLICEMAN. Do you have someone you can call?

JOE. I don't know.

POLICEMAN. Would you like to use my mobile?

JOE. I'm really embarrassed.

POLICEMAN. Have you had a fight? With your girlfriend?

JOE. I'm a walking cliché.

POLICEMAN. You shouldn't stay out here. Not on your own.

JOE. I'll call my sister.

POLICEMAN. Let me call her for you.

JOE. I'd rather call her.

POLICEMAN. Of course.

JOE. Okay

The POLICEMAN *waits.*

Can I call her myself?

POLICEMAN. I'd just rather – [wait].

JOE *gets out his mobile. He dials. He puts it to his ear, then takes it away.*

JOE. I don't have a sister.

POLICEMAN. Call someone else.

JOE. I'll just go to the campsite.

POLICEMAN. I'll follow you.

JOE. Don't you have drug dealers to arrest?

POLICEMAN. I got called to a builder's yard, Christmas Eve.
A man that worked there, he'd gone in that morning,
switched on the bulldozer, got a brick and put it on the pedal.
Then he just lay down in front of it.

Pause.

Obviously he was dead when I got there.

JOE. God.

POLICEMAN. He had some mental problems.

JOE. Well, yeah –

POLICEMAN. What?

JOE. Obviously. You wouldn't –

POLICEMAN. No.

JOE. You wouldn't do something like that if you didn't.

POLICEMAN. You wonder what was going through his mind.
Have you seen how big those things are?

JOE. Awful.

POLICEMAN. Then I get a radio about a car – smoke. And
I think, Jesus. Not two in a week.

JOE. I'm sorry.

POLICEMAN. I haven't been sleeping very well.

JOE. Didn't mean to scare you.

POLICEMAN. He lay down width-ways.

JOE. Right.

POLICEMAN. So all his guts had just popped out his sides. Reminded me of seeing a dead fox on the road.

Beat.

At least this way, there's no pain is there?

JOE. I wasn't –

POLICEMAN. I know, I know. I'm just saying. Funny thing is, this way, isn't even a way at all.

JOE. I'm not –

POLICEMAN. Well any car built in the last thirty years has a catalytic convertor doesn't it?

JOE stares blankly.

That takes out all the harmful emissions. It's actually impossible to kill yourself with car fumes these days. I still see it on telly though. It's misleading.

JOE. – Suppose it's just desperation.

POLICEMAN. Hm?

JOE. Your man – he wasn't thinking –

POLICEMAN. If he was thinking he wouldn't do it.

JOE. No.

POLICEMAN. So I'd just rather see that you were all right. I can see a car seat in the back. Why don't you go home?

JOE. We've split up.

POLICEMAN. Is that why you're sleeping in your car?

JOE. I didn't have time to get myself sorted.

POLICEMAN. There must be someone you can go to?

JOE. Can't I just stay here? It's late; I'm all set up.

POLICEMAN *hesitates.*

It's New Year's Eve. Everyone's busy.

POLICEMAN. Okay.

JOE. Thank you.

POLICEMAN. But just tonight. And listen fella, tomorrow's a new day. A new year in fact. Things are always better in the morning aren't they?

JOE *nods*.

The POLICEMAN *hesitates*.

Take care of yourself.

He leaves.

In the distance, fireworks go off.

JOE *watches them for a moment before pulling something out from under his blanket*.

It's a hosepipe.

Some months later.

A roadside café. A halfway point. It's early evening, the place is deserted. A broken light flickers every so often.

ANNE *is sitting at a table. She has a plastic cup of coffee, some photographs she's printed out, she nervously rearranges them. She's made an effort with her appearance. She's waiting, watching the door. Some time passes before* JOE *enters*.

He is dressed in a suit. He's come from work. He stops at the door as he sees ANNE.

She stands and they face each other for a moment.

Gradually he makes his way to join her.

ANNE. Hi.

  Pause.

  Suit?

He nods.

New job?

JOE. Yeah.

ANNE. What are you doing?

JOE. What do you want?

ANNE. Wow. Coffee? Mine tastes like soap –

JOE. I don't want a coffee –

ANNE. That light keeps flickering –

JOE. Why am I here, Anne?

ANNE. I – wanted to see you. I thought it was time.

JOE. Did you?

ANNE. I thought you might want to see me –

JOE. Is it about Ally?

ANNE. Of course, what else –

JOE. I haven't got long –

ANNE. Steph expecting you?

JOE. Yes.

ANNE. And the baby?

JOE. And the baby is fucking expecting me too. Yes.

ANNE. What's her name?

Beat.

It's Lola isn't it? That's lovely.

Beat.

Did everything – go okay – the birth?

JOE. Yes.

Beat.

It was good.

ANNE. That's good.

JOE. I haven't heard from you in months.

ANNE. Well – no. I wasn't allowed –

JOE. After they charged me?

Pause.

ANNE. We're not at my dad's place any more. We've not been there, for a while. Fucking Trish. Can't have her perfect – perfect life messed up. Do you know she screamed her head off once because Alistair didn't screw the milk lid on properly? My dad – My dad – he didn't even say anything. Nothing. Just sat there. Just –

She tries not to show her hurt.

Then my mum gets in touch – just out the blue. Like she does. Jet-sets in. Like she knows. Do I want to come see her? Me see her? Fat chance. Fat bloody chance.

Beat.

But – we're doing well. Got Alistair into a lovely village school. We've got a lovely apartment. I'm picking up hours at a farm shop, and a Holiday Inn just off the motorway –

JOE. Sounds perfect.

ANNE. Thinking about moving back actually.

JOE. Why?

ANNE. Wouldn't you like that?

JOE. You're going to move him out of another school?

ANNE. You haven't even asked about him?

Beat.

I've brought some recent photographs. I didn't want to message you then – in case Steph – I just thought –

She pushes them over to JOE, *but he won't look.*

Don't you even want to see?

Beat.

This is your son, Joe.

JOE. I know that.

ANNE. Don't you even care?

JOE. He doesn't want me –

ANNE. He's hurting; he's a little boy –

JOE. You can't –

He glares at her.

Beat.

ANNE. We were always arguing. Always like this. Just our way. Amount of times you slept in the shed. Just – us. We'd scream and we'd fight and then we'd make up. Sometimes you'd do that thing – knock on the coffee table, and look at me. 'Knock, knock.' And eventually – I'd knock back.

Beat.

After you left –

JOE. You kicked me out.

ANNE. I was always kicking you out.

JOE. Put all my stuff in suitcases. Nothing was ripped or shredded. It was all neatly packed.

ANNE. I kept waiting for the knock.

Beat.

One week. Two weeks. I thought – he's making show of this.

Beat.

You said you couldn't imagine your life without me.

Beat.

I've been reading lots of books. Yoga. It's just closure. That's all. Healthy – good to say things. God. I feel so much better saying it.

Pause.

JOE. When Ally was born –

ANNE. Alistair.

JOE. Fucking Alistair then.

ANNE. His friends keep calling him Ally.

JOE. When he was born – when they thought – when they told us, he was gone. I was frozen. Felt frozen the whole time, everyone rushing round, no idea what was going on. Like having front-row seats to watch the people you love most in a car crash.

Beat.

You said 'Give him to me.' You made them. You just knew exactly what to do. Like this was what you were meant for.

She smiles.

Overwhelmed by the comment.

I – struggled – Once – Once I was in the supermarket, and someone was cleaning the floor and all I could think of was the smell of that delivery suite, and I just dropped my shopping and left.

ANNE. Did you?

JOE. Felt like a failed him. He'd only been alive a few moments, and already –

Beat.

Promised him – never again. Used to drive you mad, didn't I? Way I was every time he got sick. Didn't want to leave his side.

Beat.

After – what happened? Couldn't get my head around it. Kept seeing his little face – way he looked at me in the woods. Thinking about my own dad. Thinking about how scared I used to be of him.

JOE *is holding in the emotion.*

– I don't remember – He tried to run. I grabbed hold of him –

ANNE *pushes the photographs to* JOE *again.*

ANNE. Just look at him. He's growing up so much –

JOE. I can't

ANNE. What do you mean?

JOE. I've got a family now –

ANNE. He's your family –

JOE. You don't know –

ANNE. He misses you –

JOE. I thought I was going to court – You told them – *he* told them –

ANNE. You frightened him.

JOE. Did I do those marks? I just held on to him – maybe I held on tight?

ANNE. He gets so angry sometimes, Joe. I don't know where it comes from. One minute he won't leave my side, the next he's throwing things round in his room. I'm worried about him getting in with the wrong type. I know that sounds mad. But he follows this boy around everywhere. He just so easily impressed. He needs you. He's taken some time and – and he's ready now. He's ready, Joe. He wants to meet his little sister. I could drop him here. You could pick him up –

JOE *is shaking his head.*

You can't do this to him. He'll never forgive you.

JOE. Can't.

ANNE. Can't – what? What the fuck are you talking about? This is your son. Because of her?

JOE. It's not

ANNE. You're putting them first?

JOE. You fucking – wreck everything –

ANNE. Oh here we go –

JOE. *You*, Anne –

ANNE. You need to take some responsibility –

JOE. You called the fucking police –

ANNE. You took him –

JOE. How can you take your own son?

ANNE. I had no idea where he was –

JOE. Did I hurt him?

ANNE. I was worried sick.

JOE *is leaving – she getting up to stop him.*

You should have listened to me –

JOE. Get out my way –

ANNE. That's all I ever wanted –

JOE. This is what you wanted –

ANNE. / I'm the mother of your child –

JOE. Get out my fucking way –

ANNE. You're not leaving –

He pushes past her.

You can't do this. You don't know what it does.

Long pause.

JOE. I drove my car out on New Year's Eve. After everything. Christmas – Christmas without him – it just all – And Steph was calling round everyone. She was nine months' pregnant and I put her through that. I was sat in my car. I could just feel it. I could feel it all in my – in my – I just wanted it to stop.

Beat.

We have a daughter now. I can't let myself – go back there. I'm doing better now.

ANNE. You won't do this.

Beat.

I know you – you won't.

JOE. What if this is the best thing for Ally?

ANNE. What? Leave – ?

JOE. Yes.

ANNE. He needs his dad –

JOE. He needs this?

Pause.

ANNE. You took me camping. When we first started dating –
you made me hike to this spot. I was sweating – remember?
I was practically on the verge of tears. Except you kept
singing – (*Sings.*) 'I would walk five hundred miles and
I would walk five hundred more' – in this – this really bad
Scottish accent. And what was that lyric you kept – instead
of 'da da da da'. You said – you said?

Beat.

What did you say? Joe – ?

JOE. Hannibal Lecter –

ANNE (*sings*). Hannibal Lecter. Hannibal Lecter.

JOE (*sings*). – Hannibal Lecter.

ANNE. That's it. And I was like it's not 'Hannibal Lecter'.
Why would he say 'Hannibal Lecter?' I couldn't stop
laughing. And it was so hot. And the place was full of
midges. And even when we finally managed to set up the tent
there were thousands of them inside. You'd literally flick
your lighter and hear them sizzle on the end of the flame.
You gave me the sleeping bag with the drawstring so I could
cover myself up – and you had the shitty Asda one I bought.
And we were still laughing about 'Hannibal Lecter' in the
darkness. (*Sings, softly, remembering.*) Hannibal Lecter.

Beat.

In the morning you looked like a complete mutant.

She laughs – through tears. JOE *is still trying to hold it in.*

Pause.

I told Alistair that story. He loved hearing it.

Beat.

Of course, I had to explain who Hannibal Lecter was.

Beat.

I want – want him to know the good bits too, Joe. He has to. He has to know us.

A moment.

JOE *leaves suddenly.*

ANNE *isn't sure what to do.*

He returns – he's holding 'Pinky' the teddy bear.

Is that?

JOE. It's not the same one. I had to go online. A lot of searching. It's new.

ANNE *holds it too for a moment.*

It's been in my car.

Pause.

ANNE. We can do better – can't we?

They watch each other.

The light is flickering –

Sometimes –

Sometimes –

People just fall –

Love is like a plant.

It happens.

Our love was gone –

Watering –

If you don't water it –

There might not be any big reason –

Love is gone.

They don't love each other any more.

That made us feel –

You have to look after your love –

Disappeared completely –

One day we realised –

Disappeared –

How hard we tried.

Never ever go away.

Different sort of love.

Love that needs watering –

This isn't your fault.

Anything wrong.

For the best.

We won't –

We'll be –

Better.

Possible –

Better –

Normal.

Okay –

Okay?

We promise.

We love you.

More –

Bigger –

Bigger than this.

The light flickers to a stop.

www.nickhernbooks.co.uk

facebook.com/nickhernbooks

twitter.com/nickhernbooks